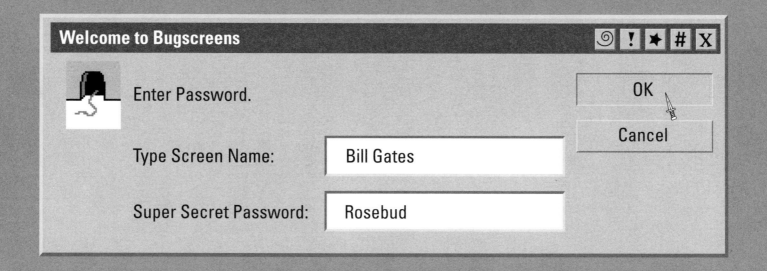

Microspoof

Microspoof
Bugscreens 98

My Laptop

My Piggy Bank

My Shredder

Shit Can

Death Ray

Launch Codes

My Laptop

My Piggy Bank

My Shredder

Shit Can

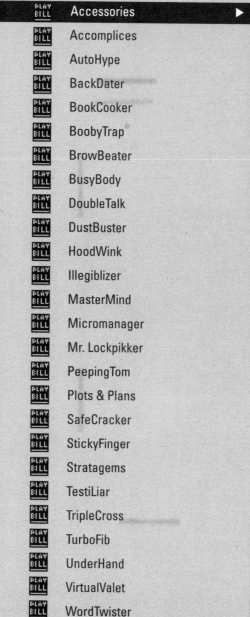

PLAY BILL	**Accessories** ▶
PLAY BILL	Accomplices
PLAY BILL	AutoHype
PLAY BILL	BackDater
PLAY BILL	BookCooker
PLAY BILL	BoobyTrap
PLAY BILL	BrowBeater
PLAY BILL	BusyBody
PLAY BILL	DoubleTalk
PLAY BILL	DustBuster
PLAY BILL	HoodWink
PLAY BILL	Illegiblizer
PLAY BILL	MasterMind
PLAY BILL	Micromanager
PLAY BILL	Mr. Lockpikker
PLAY BILL	PeepingTom
PLAY BILL	Plots & Plans
PLAY BILL	SafeCracker
PLAY BILL	StickyFinger
PLAY BILL	Stratagems
PLAY BILL	TestiLiar
PLAY BILL	TripleCross
PLAY BILL	TurboFib
PLAY BILL	UnderHand
PLAY BILL	VirtualValet
PLAY BILL	WordTwister

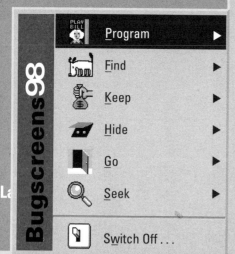

PLAY BILL	**Program**	▶
	Find	▶
	Keep	▶
	Hide	▶
	Go	▶
	Seek	▶
	Switch Off . . .	

Bugscreens 98

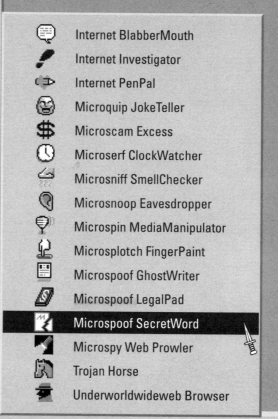

	Internet BlabberMouth
	Internet Investigator
	Internet PenPal
	Microquip JokeTeller
	Microscam Excess
	Microserf ClockWatcher
	Microsniff SmellChecker
	Microsnoop Eavesdropper
	Microspin MediaManipulator
	Microsplotch FingerPaint
	Microspoof GhostWriter
	Microspoof LegalPad
	Microspoof SecretWord
	Microspy Web Prowler
	Trojan Horse
	Underworldwideweb Browser

La

⊞ Begin

12:12 PM

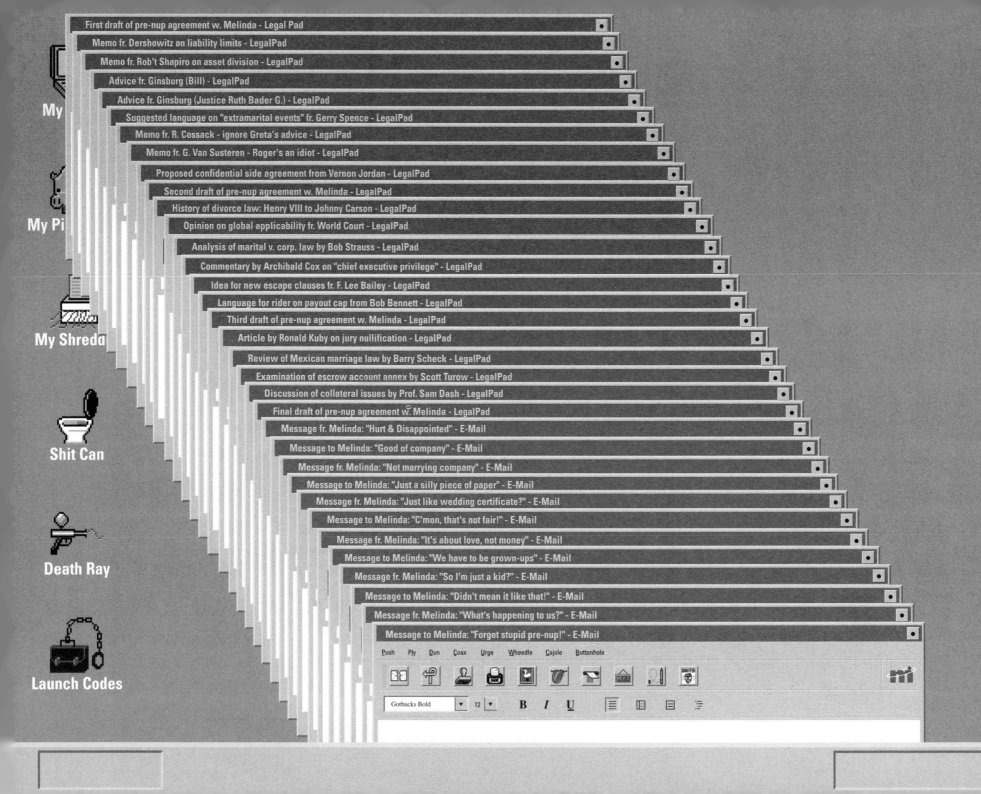

Microspoof SecretWord ◎ ! ★ # X

Fail   Erase   Crash   Freeze   Fault   Bugs   Trouble   Error   Dump

Gotbucks Bold ▼   10 ▼

Make-over

L | | | | | 1 | | | | | | 2 | | | | | | 3 L | | | | | 4 | | | | | | 5 | | | | | 6 | | | | ▲

Everybody Hates Me - Time to Remake Image - Kinder & Gentler Bill!

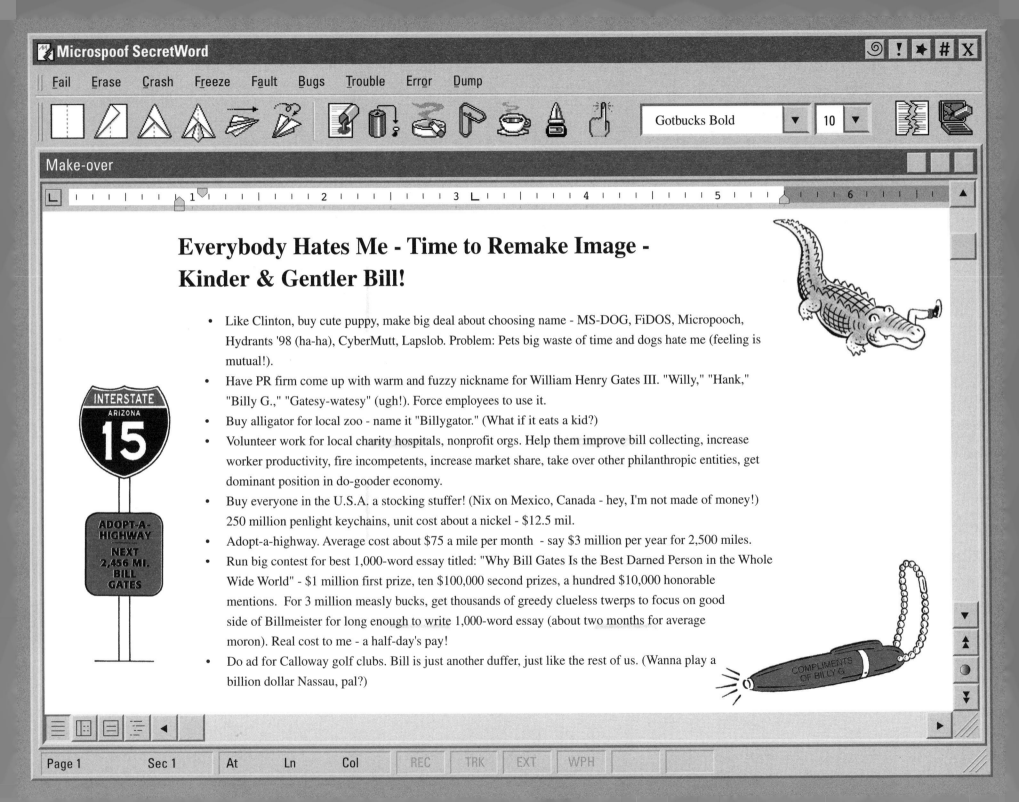

- Like Clinton, buy cute puppy, make big deal about choosing name - MS-DOG, FiDOS, Micropooch, Hydrants '98 (ha-ha), CyberMutt, Lapslob. Problem: Pets big waste of time and dogs hate me (feeling is mutual!).
- Have PR firm come up with warm and fuzzy nickname for William Henry Gates III. "Willy," "Hank," "Billy G.," "Gatesy-watesy" (ugh!). Force employees to use it.
- Buy alligator for local zoo - name it "Billygator." (What if it eats a kid?)
- Volunteer work for local charity hospitals, nonprofit orgs. Help them improve bill collecting, increase worker productivity, fire incompetents, increase market share, take over other philanthropic entities, get dominant position in do-gooder economy.
- Buy everyone in the U.S.A. a stocking stuffer! (Nix on Mexico, Canada - hey, I'm not made of money!) 250 million penlight keychains, unit cost about a nickel - $12.5 mil.
- Adopt-a-highway. Average cost about $75 a mile per month - say $3 million per year for 2,500 miles.
- Run big contest for best 1,000-word essay titled: "Why Bill Gates Is the Best Darned Person in the Whole Wide World" - $1 million first prize, ten $100,000 second prizes, a hundred $10,000 honorable mentions. For 3 million measly bucks, get thousands of greedy clueless twerps to focus on good side of Billmeister for long enough to write 1,000-word essay (about two months for average moron). Real cost to me - a half-day's pay!
- Do ad for Calloway golf clubs. Bill is just another duffer, just like the rest of us. (Wanna play a billion dollar Nassau, pal?)

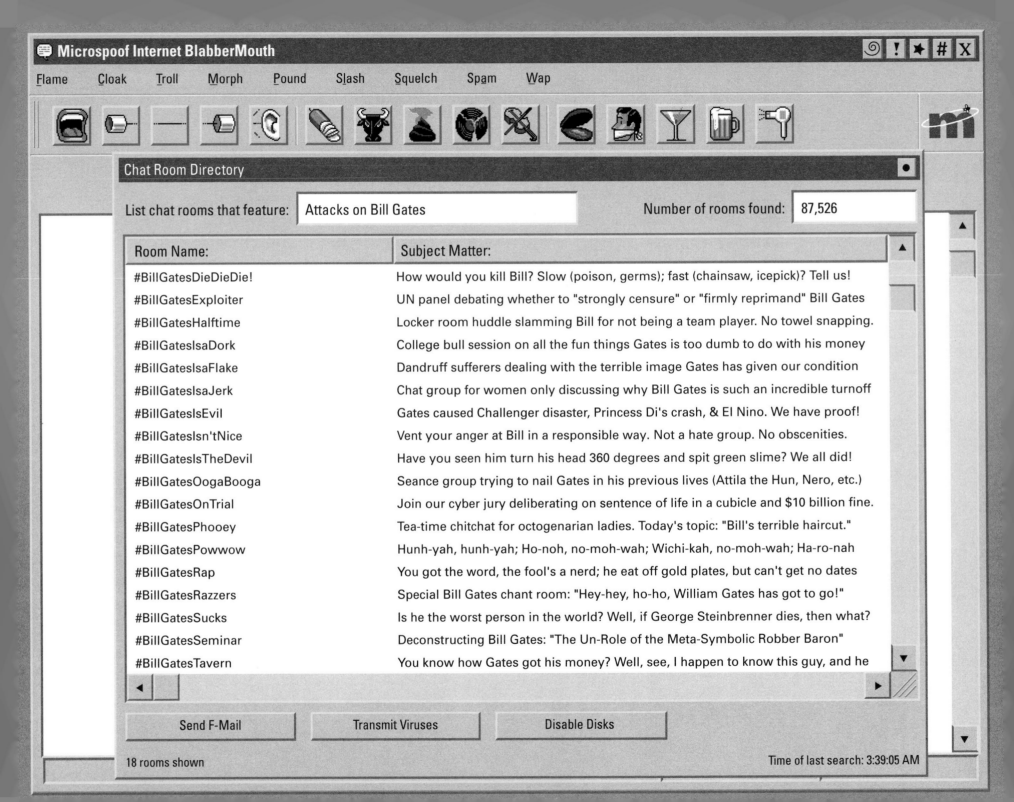

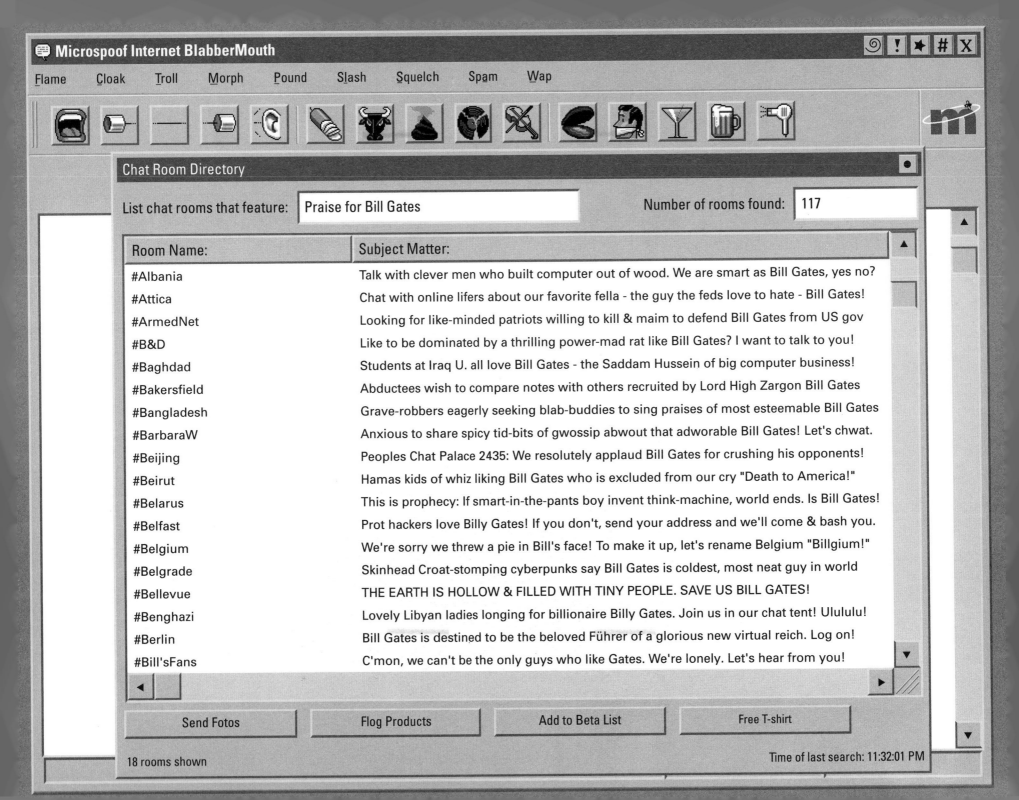

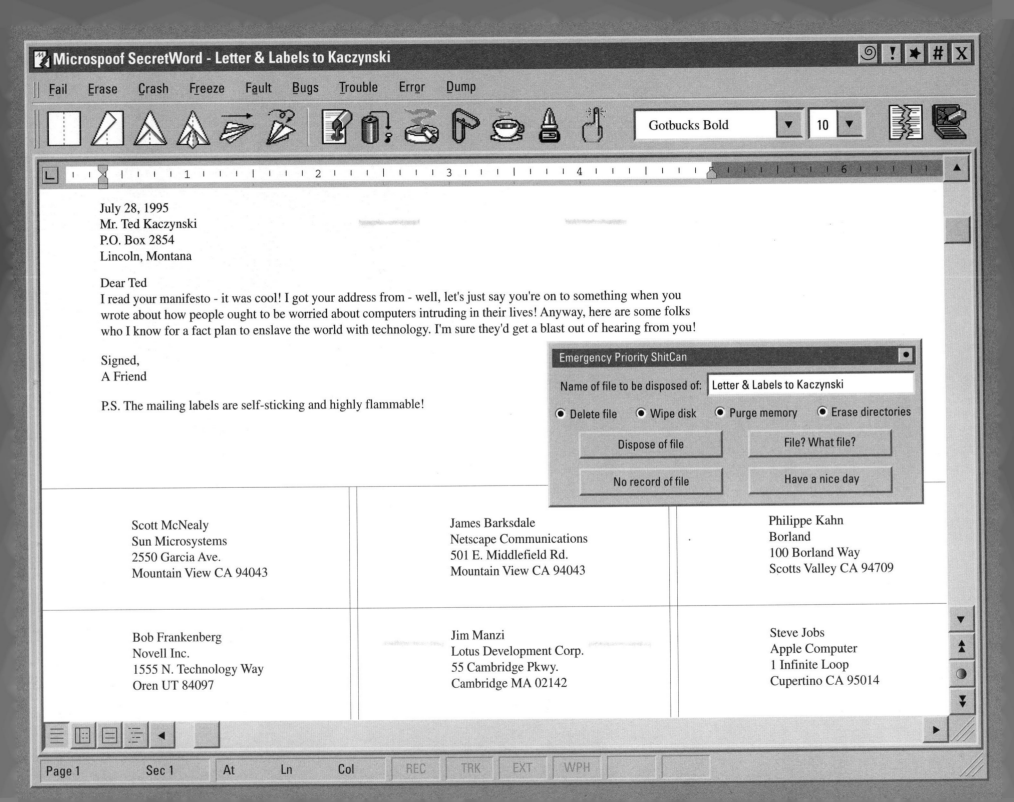

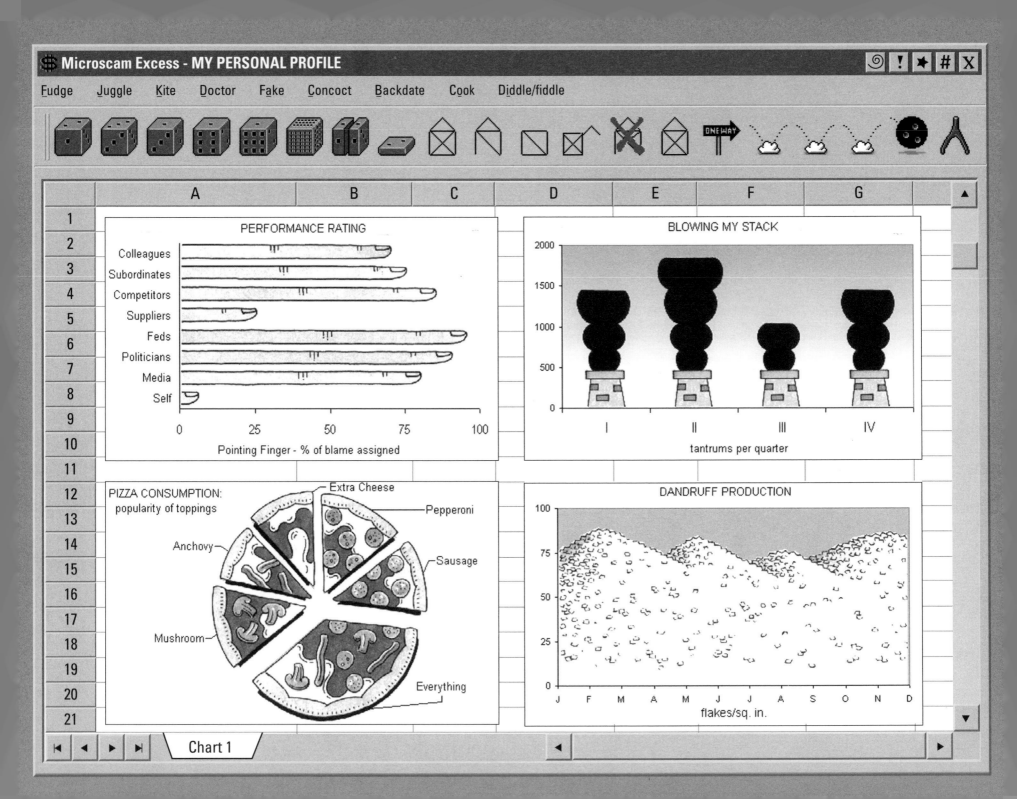

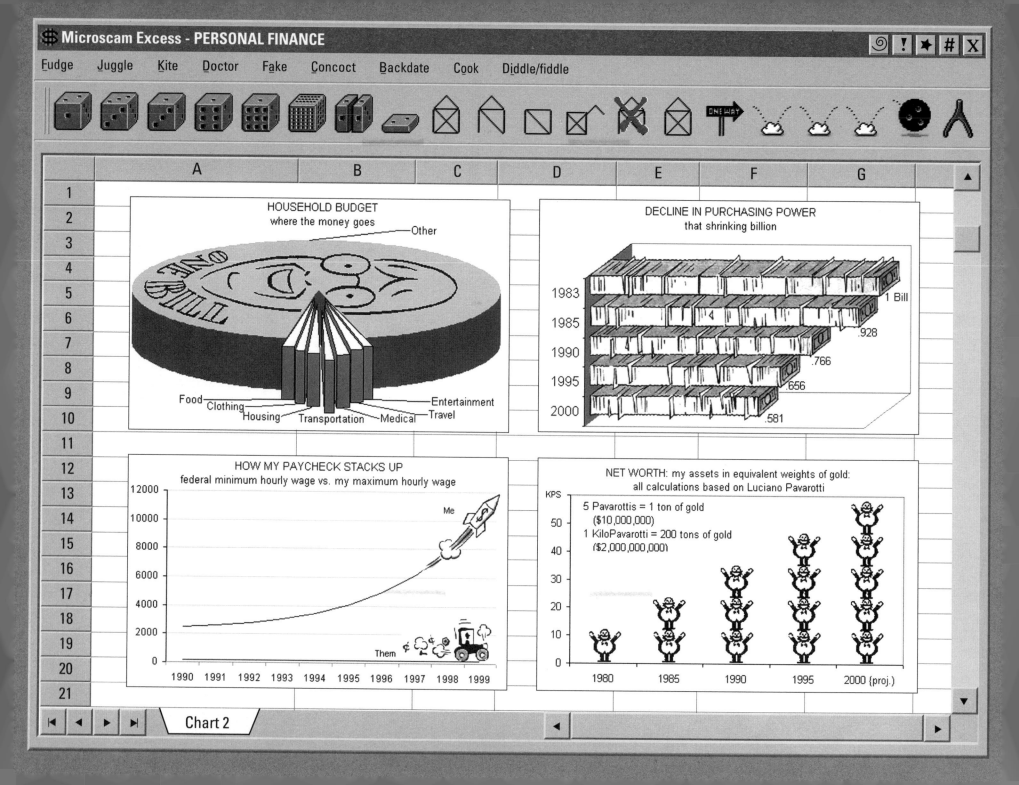

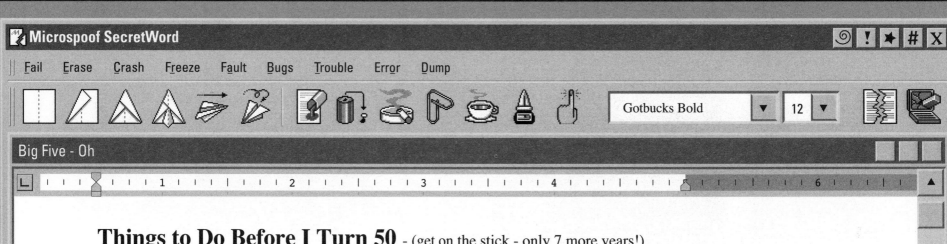

Microspoof SecretWord

Fail   Erase   Crash   Freeze   Fault   Bugs   Trouble   Error   Dump

Gotbucks Bold   ▼   12   ▼

Big Five - Oh

Things to Do Before I Turn 50 - (get on the stick - only 7 more years!)

- play racquetball in Sistine Chapel
  (with Pope, if guy isn't half dead)
- play round of golf with Arnold Palmer at St. Andrews
  (Steve Jobs caddies!)
- 4 for bridge: Me, Warren Buffett, Dalai Lama, Stephen Hawking
  (need drool-proof deck)
- game of catch with J. D. Salinger
- waterski on River Ganges (make sure to get vaccinations,
  avoid untouchables - use disposable skis)
- gold record of me doing karaoke version of "Feelings"
  (easy to sell a million, just bundle it with Windows 98 -
  they gotta buy it!)
- my face on Mt. Rushmore
  (with glasses? little boulders for dandruff?)
- cut off tippy-top of Mt. Everest and put in back yard -
  climb it any time I feel like it!
- get comet named after me (talk to Hale and Bopp -
  may do deal on theirs)
- get cloned now!
  William Henry Gates III, Version 4.0, before big 5 - 0!

Page 1   Sec 1   At   Ln   Col   REC   TRK   EXT   WPH

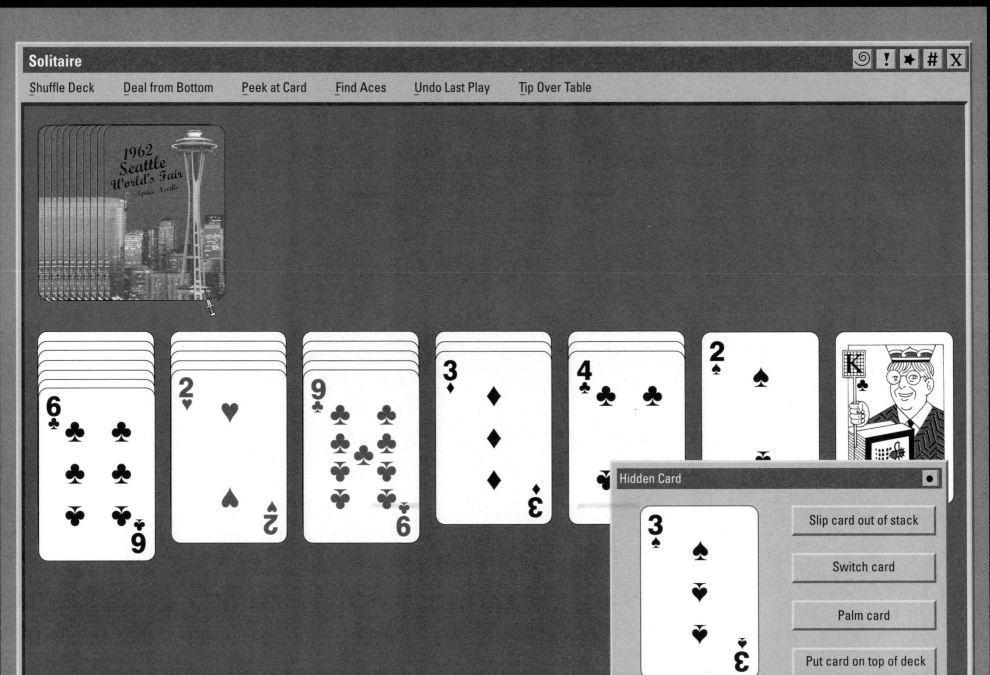

Target

Dig

Hide

Safecrack

Wiretap

Bury File

Switch
Rummage

Address: http://fbi.gov/www.html   Links

Defeat Encryption | Password Bypass | Activate Buried Access Program

GATES, WILLIAM H. III   **SECRET**   **PAGE 46**

enormous success has provided very significant levels of medium- to
high-compensation employment in the Pacific Northwest and has, as well,
placed the United States in a preeminent position as a competitive force
in the international software market, with concomitant benefits to the
national balance of trade, Gates remains a serious threat to domestic
competitors and possibly to the U.S. Government as well. His predatory
tactics may have a mid- to long-term negative impact on national security
by discouraging innovation in this critical field in the years to come,
and the extraordinary penetration his products have achieved in government
and in the private sector raise pressing issues about the confidentiality
of data in virtually every computer in use today.

CONCLUSIONS

William H. Gates is a wonderful guy and a darn fine American. Everyone
in the F.B.I. should do everything in their power to help him and, at the
same time, screw his enemies royally.

**Mr. Lockpikker
wants to know
what you want
him to do?**

- Insert data
- Remove data
- Copy data
- Alter data

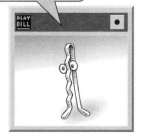

X Enough Already   J. Edgar Zone

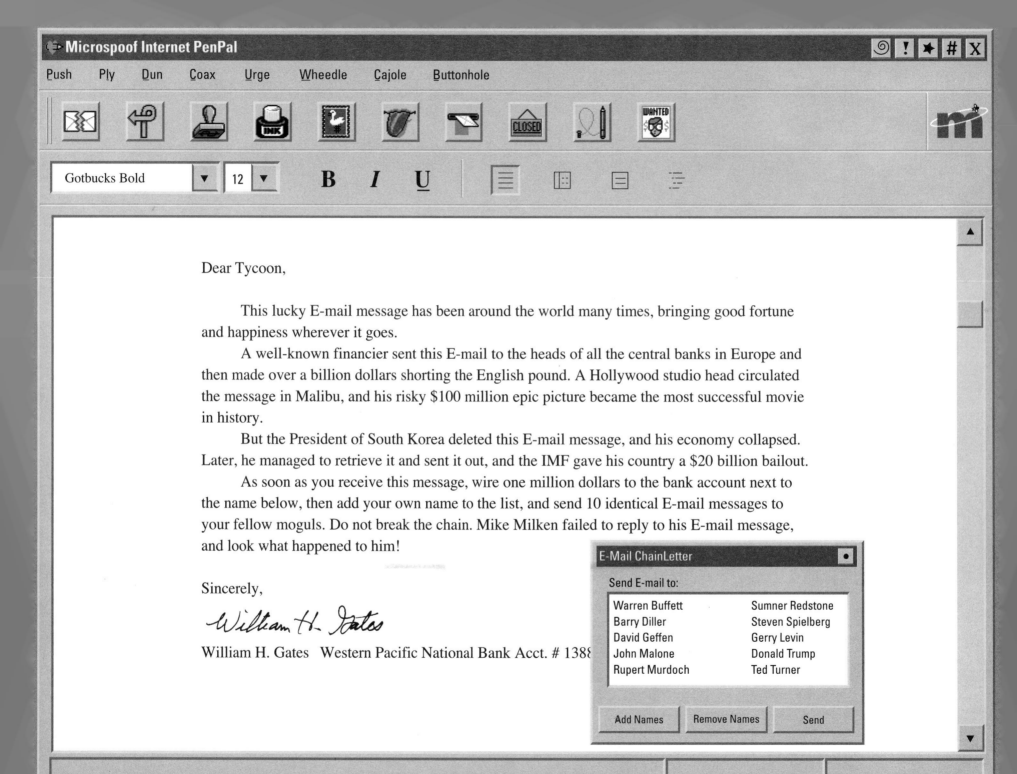

Microspoof Internet PenPal

Push   Ply   Dun   Coax   Urge   Wheedle   Cajole   Buttonhole

Gotbucks Bold   12   **B** *I* <u>U</u>

Dear Tycoon,

This lucky E-mail message has been around the world many times, bringing good fortune and happiness wherever it goes.

A well-known financier sent this E-mail to the heads of all the central banks in Europe and then made over a billion dollars shorting the English pound. A Hollywood studio head circulated the message in Malibu, and his risky $100 million epic picture became the most successful movie in history.

But the President of South Korea deleted this E-mail message, and his economy collapsed. Later, he managed to retrieve it and sent it out, and the IMF gave his country a $20 billion bailout.

As soon as you receive this message, wire one million dollars to the bank account next to the name below, then add your own name to the list, and send 10 identical E-mail messages to your fellow moguls. Do not break the chain. Mike Milken failed to reply to his E-mail message, and look what happened to him!

Sincerely,

William H. Gates

William H. Gates   Western Pacific National Bank Acct. # 1388

E-Mail ChainLetter

Send E-mail to:

Warren Buffett	Sumner Redstone
Barry Diller	Steven Spielberg
David Geffen	Gerry Levin
John Malone	Donald Trump
Rupert Murdoch	Ted Turner

Add Names   Remove Names   Send

Microspoof SecretWord

Fail   Erase   Crash   Freeze   Fault   Bugs   Trouble   Error   Dump

Gotbucks Bold   10

Big Ideas

L   1   2   3   4   6

Possible New Software Products

(NOTE: don't release until after fed. anti-trust suit is settled)

- **Plagiarizer** - uses pre-programmed Thesaurus to change random nouns, adjectives, and adverbs in any text. Copyright-Killer!

- **Bars-on-Windows 98 accounting programs** - ideal for white-collar criminals. Includes BookCooker spreadsheet, BackDater document faker, Bamboozle number-scrambler, and TurboFib and Alibi excuse-making options.

- **Resume-Expander** - massages personal biographies to improve impact. Automatically corrects obvious inconsistencies, intrinsically unbelievable claims.

- **Cubicle 98 office politics software** - BackStabber memo-writing program with BlameShifter feature and FingerPointer mouse hardware; also, PaperShuffler screen-saver program to make workstations appear to be in use.

- **Internet programs** - Black E-Mail with untraceable source code, special type fonts; ChainLetter pyramid-scheme document generators; CrankMail letter-writing program for creating blizzard of nut notes to congressmen, etc.

- **Microscrooge letter-writing program** - automatically generates rejection letters turning down appeals for donations from charities.

Microspoof SecretWord

You have entered a command which has defrosted your refrigerator.

Okay

Page 1   Sec 1   At   Ln   Col   REC   TRK   EXT   WPH

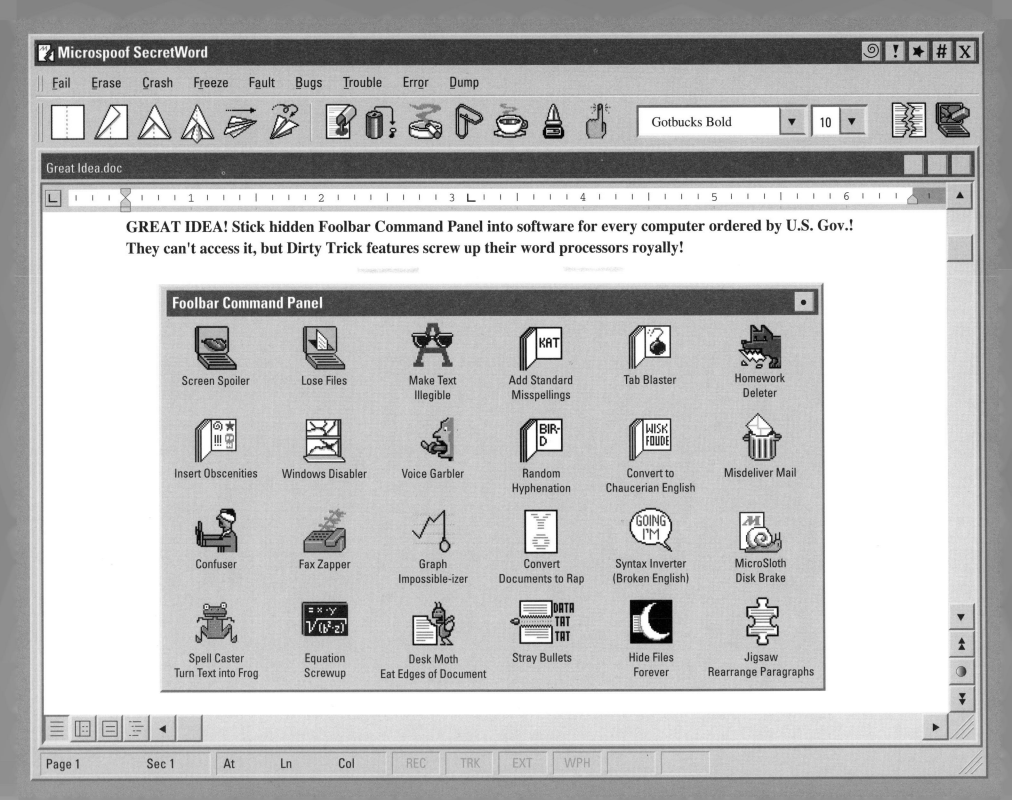

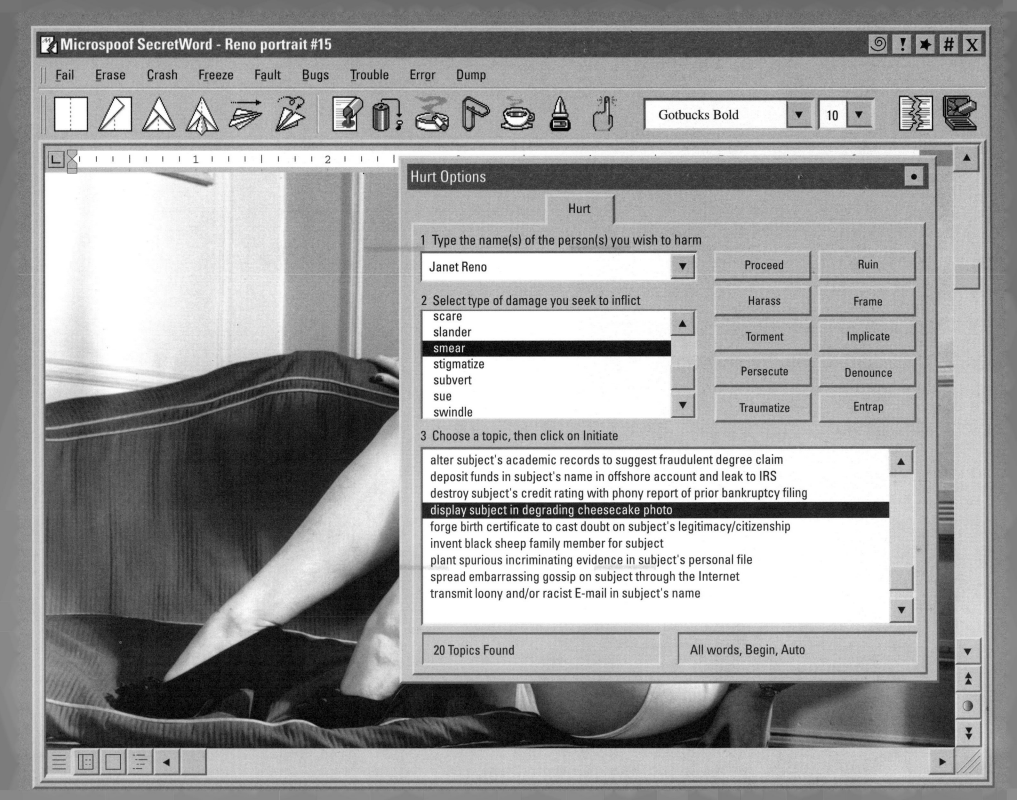

Microspoof SecretWord - Reno portrait #15

Fail Erase Crash Freeze Fault Bugs Trouble Error Dump

Gotbucks Bold ▼ 10 ▼

L | | | | 1 | | | | | | 2 | | | |

Hurt Options

Hurt

1 Type the name(s) of the person(s) you wish to harm

Janet Reno ▼

2 Select type of damage you seek to inflict

- scare
- slander
- **smear**
- stigmatize
- subvert
- sue
- swindle

Proceed	Ruin
Harass	Frame
Torment	Implicate
Persecute	Denounce
Traumatize	Entrap

3 Choose a topic, then click on Initiate

- alter subject's academic records to suggest fraudulent degree claim
- deposit funds in subject's name in offshore account and leak to IRS
- destroy subject's credit rating with phony report of prior bankruptcy filing
- **display subject in degrading cheesecake photo**
- forge birth certificate to cast doubt on subject's legitimacy/citizenship
- invent black sheep family member for subject
- plant spurious incriminating evidence in subject's personal file
- spread embarrassing gossip on subject through the Internet
- transmit loony and/or racist E-mail in subject's name

20 Topics Found

All words, Begin, Auto

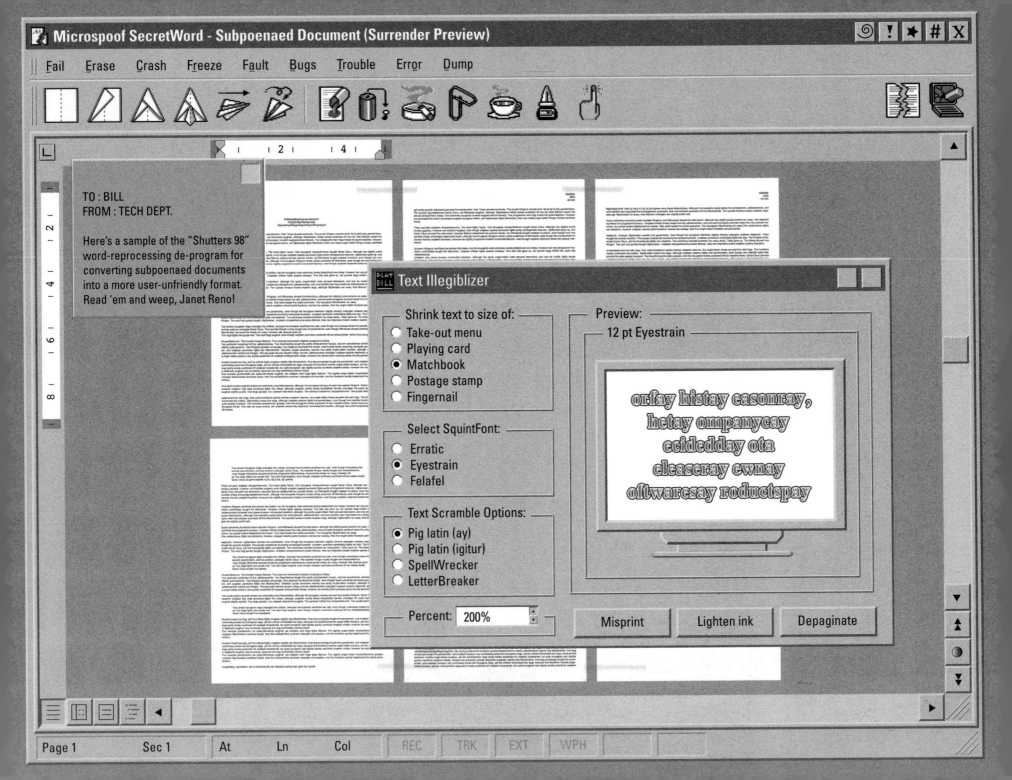

Fail   Erase   Crash   Freeze   Fault   Bugs   Trouble   Error   Dump

Gotbucks Bold   ▼   11 ▼

STATEMENT FOR SENATE HEARING   VERSION 1

Let me begin by saying what a royal pain in the ass it is to come to this useless crime-ridden scuzzbucket of a city just so I can sit here while a bunch of pompous two-faced gasbags can take time off from robbing the country blind and sucking up to the morons who were dumb enough to vote for you just long enough to give me a hard time for creating the most successful company in the history of the world.

If I'd had the brains to slip you sleazeballs a few million bucks like most of my crybaby competitors did, I wouldn't be sitting here getting reamed by mealy-mouthed brain-dead moochers whose opinion of me and my company I frankly do not give a rat's patootie for. As far as I'm concerned, all of you can go take a flying fuck at a rolling donut. If any of you dimwits held an actual job

---

STATEMENT FOR SENATE HEARING   VERSION 2

Let me begin by saying that I am happy to come to Washington today to meet with our nation's distinguished elected representatives. I am grateful to have this opportunity to appear before you in person to address some of the issues and concerns that have been expressed recently, both in the media and by our government, regarding competition and market practices in the software industry.

I welcome the chance to respond directly to some of the accusations and criticisms leveled at our corporation by industry analysts and our competitors, and to assure you that our actions have always been motivated, and will always continue to be guided, by our commitment to innovation and our desire to provide our customers with the best possible products at the lowest possible price

---

Prod Nag Berate Rebuke Ream Wangle Finesse Delegate Turf Angles Regroup Circumvent Rectify

Simple List ▼

Actions

Chits

Paybacks

Game Plan

Nit Picks

Brainstorm

Reprimand

Pink Slip

To-do List for Contractor

✓	✓✓	Subject
		Make aquarium bigger - giant clam, larger fish (swordfish, tuna), actual castle, real diver
		Great hall too empty-looking - lose suits of armor and banners, get dinosaur and Titanic replica
		Water bed is cool! Find water sofa, water desk, water drapes, water credenza!
		Make sure to leave room in garage for muffler and transmission shop and state inspection station
		Statue of me as Napoleon looks stupid - c'mon, dummies, Napoleon didn't wear glasses!
		Tiffany lamps in library too dim - try halogen bulbs. (Note - see if maybe Cartier makes lamps)
		Add carousel to baby's room. New? Turn-of-century? Star Wars characters? Check with Lucas
		Door chimes are screwed up. I ordered "Winchester Cathedral" not "Eleanor Rigby"
		Call McDonald's re franchise in kitchen. Milk shakes too frothy, French fries still soggy
		Tell I. M. Pei to include heated nest, Jacuzzi, and worm dispenser in birdhouse design
		Shag carpeting too shaggy, but 20,000 sq. ft. is a lot to rip out. Can we mow it?
		See if International Date Line can be moved to run through middle of living room
		Buy Kaczynski's cabin to use as shed for pool heater, pump, filter, etc.
		Waterski jump in indoor pool not high enough - raise it at least 4 feet
		Great idea - use stock certificates of bankrupt rivals' companies as wallpaper in den!
		Hire artist to do fresco of happy domestic workers for ceiling of nanny's room
		Tile work in car wash is sloppy. Also, I specified marble floor, not terrazzo
		Solid gold spacemaker washer-dryer in guest suite looks tacky. Use platinum instead?
		TV dish only gets 500 channels. Launch own satellite?

19 Items

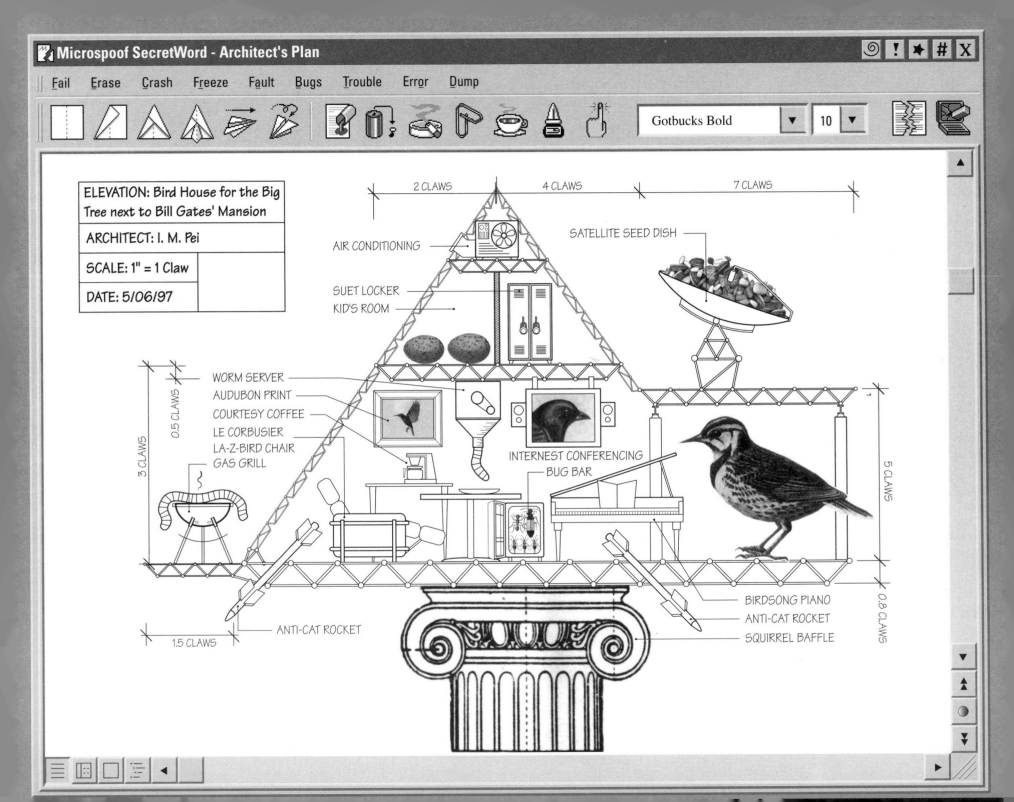

Microspoof SecretWord - Architect's Plan

Fail   Erase   Crash   Freeze   Fault   Bugs   Trouble   Error   Dump

Gotbucks Bold   10

ELEVATION: Bird House for the Big
Tree next to Bill Gates' Mansion

ARCHITECT: I. M. Pei

SCALE: 1" = 1 Claw

DATE: 5/06/97

2 CLAWS   4 CLAWS   7 CLAWS

AIR CONDITIONING

SATELLITE SEED DISH

SUET LOCKER
KID'S ROOM

WORM SERVER
AUDUBON PRINT
COURTESY COFFEE
LE CORBUSIER
LA-Z-BIRD CHAIR
GAS GRILL

INTERNEST CONFERENCING

BUG BAR

0.5 CLAWS

3 CLAWS

5 CLAWS

BIRDSONG PIANO
ANTI-CAT ROCKET
SQUIRREL BAFFLE

0.8 CLAWS

ANTI-CAT ROCKET

1.5 CLAWS

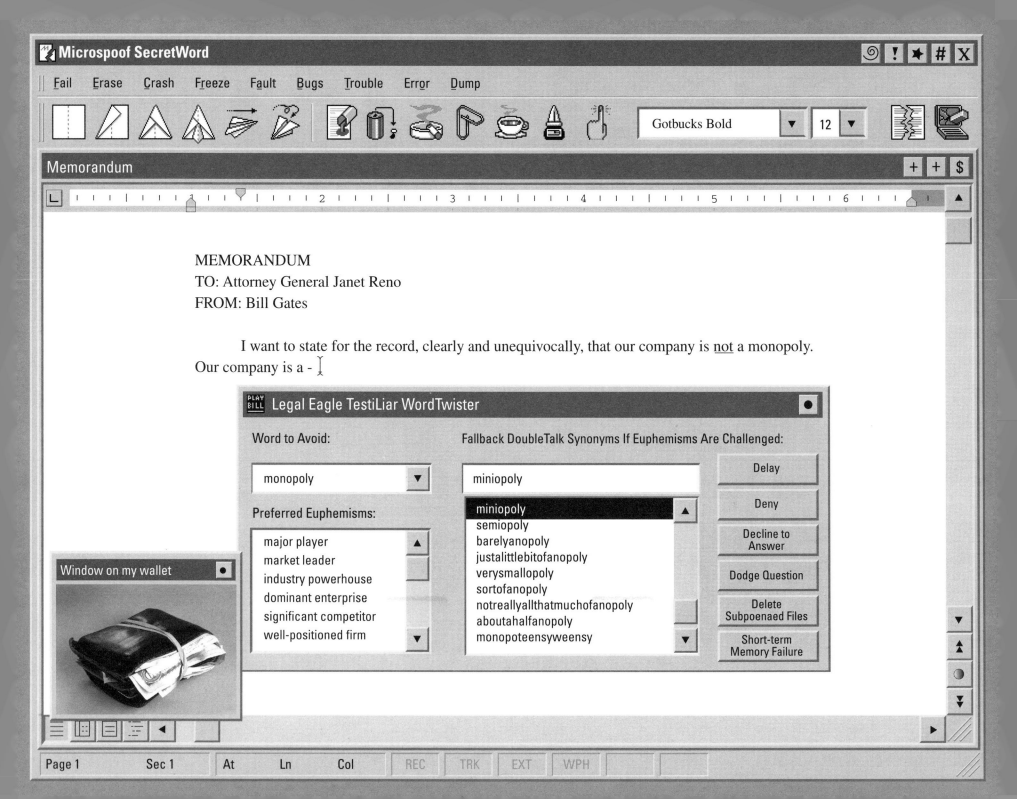

Microspoof SecretWord

Fail   Erase   Crash   Freeze   Fault   Bugs   Trouble   Error   Dump

Gotbucks Bold   ▼   12   ▼

Memorandum   + + $

MEMORANDUM
TO: Attorney General Janet Reno
FROM: Bill Gates

   I want to state for the record, clearly and unequivocally, that our company is <u>not</u> a monopoly.
Our company is a -

Legal Eagle TestiLiar WordTwister

Word to Avoid:

monopoly   ▼

Preferred Euphemisms:

major player
market leader
industry powerhouse
dominant enterprise
significant competitor
well-positioned firm

Fallback DoubleTalk Synonyms If Euphemisms Are Challenged:

miniopoly

miniopoly
semiopoly
barelyanopoly
justalittlebitofanopoly
verysmallopoly
sortofanopoly
notreallyallthatmuchofanopoly
aboutahalfanopoly
monopoteensyweensy

Delay

Deny

Decline to
Answer

Dodge Question

Delete
Subpoenaed Files

Short-term
Memory Failure

Window on my wallet

Page 1   Sec 1   At   Ln   Col   REC   TRK   EXT   WPH

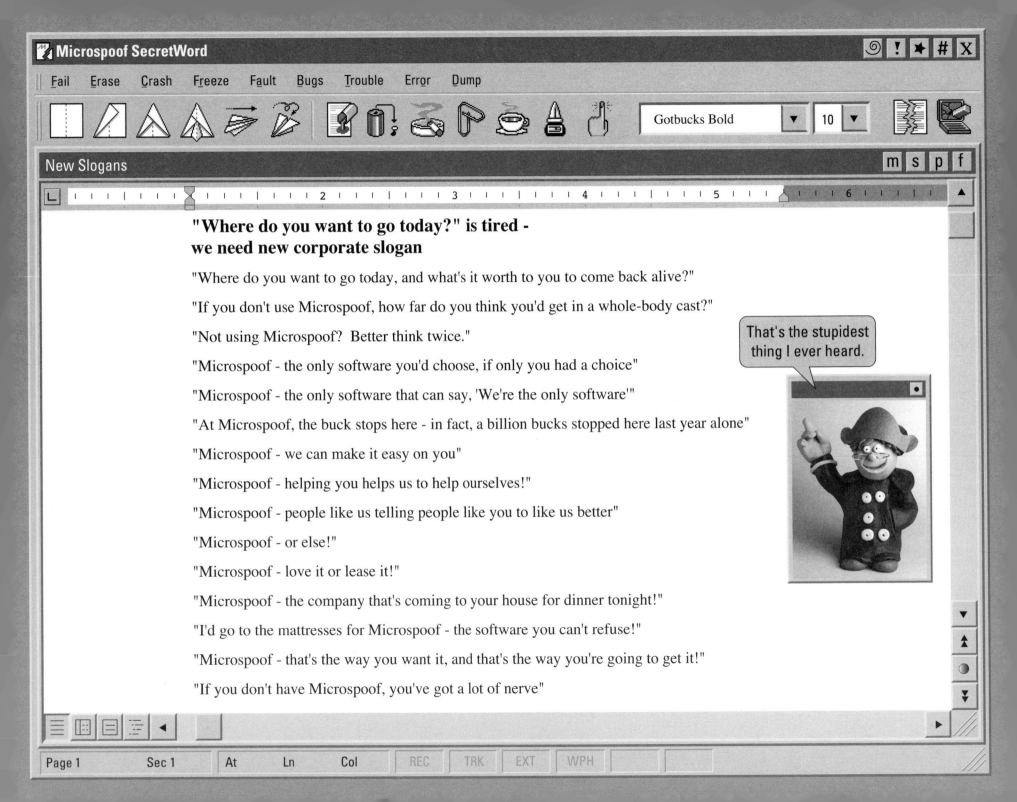

Microspoof SecretWord

Fail Erase Crash Freeze Fault Bugs Trouble Error Dump

Gotbucks Bold   10

New Slogans

"Where do you want to go today?" is tired - we need new corporate slogan

"Where do you want to go today, and what's it worth to you to come back alive?"

"If you don't use Microspoof, how far do you think you'd get in a whole-body cast?"

"Not using Microspoof? Better think twice."

"Microspoof - the only software you'd choose, if only you had a choice"

"Microspoof - the only software that can say, 'We're the only software'"

"At Microspoof, the buck stops here - in fact, a billion bucks stopped here last year alone"

"Microspoof - we can make it easy on you"

"Microspoof - helping you helps us to help ourselves!"

"Microspoof - people like us telling people like you to like us better"

"Microspoof - or else!"

"Microspoof - love it or lease it!"

"Microspoof - the company that's coming to your house for dinner tonight!"

"I'd go to the mattresses for Microspoof - the software you can't refuse!"

"Microspoof - that's the way you want it, and that's the way you're going to get it!"

"If you don't have Microspoof, you've got a lot of nerve"

That's the stupidest thing I ever heard.

Page 1   Sec 1   At   Ln   Col   REC   TRK   EXT   WPH

Microspoof Underworldwideweb Browser

Fix Extort Skim Suborn Tamper Reach Clip Ice Waste

Break	Enter	Stomp	Alias	Hideout	Muscle	Rackets	Mouthpiece	Blackmail	Hush money

Address http:// uwww.lacosanostra.crime.org   Links

MADE - TO - MEASURE

CEMENT SUIT

CLICK ON AN ICON TO SELECT DESIRED SERVICE.

The Mafia

Hey, You're Like Family to Us!

 PLACE A SPORTS BET

 LAUNDER MONEY

 LAUNCH A VENDETTA

 PLAY A NUMBER

 OBTAIN PROTECTION

 PURCHASE PHARMACEUTICAL PRODUCTS

 PROCURE A HOOKER

 BUY BARGAIN MERCHANDISE

 DISCOURAGE UNWANTED COMPETITION

 RENT A HARD-CORE FILM

 DISPOSE OF STOLEN GOODS

 SHAKE DOWN A SUPPLIER

 ARRANGE AN UNSECURED LOAN

 DISPENSE WITH CUSTOMS FORMALITIES

 SETTLE A SCORE

X Terminated   Mob Zone

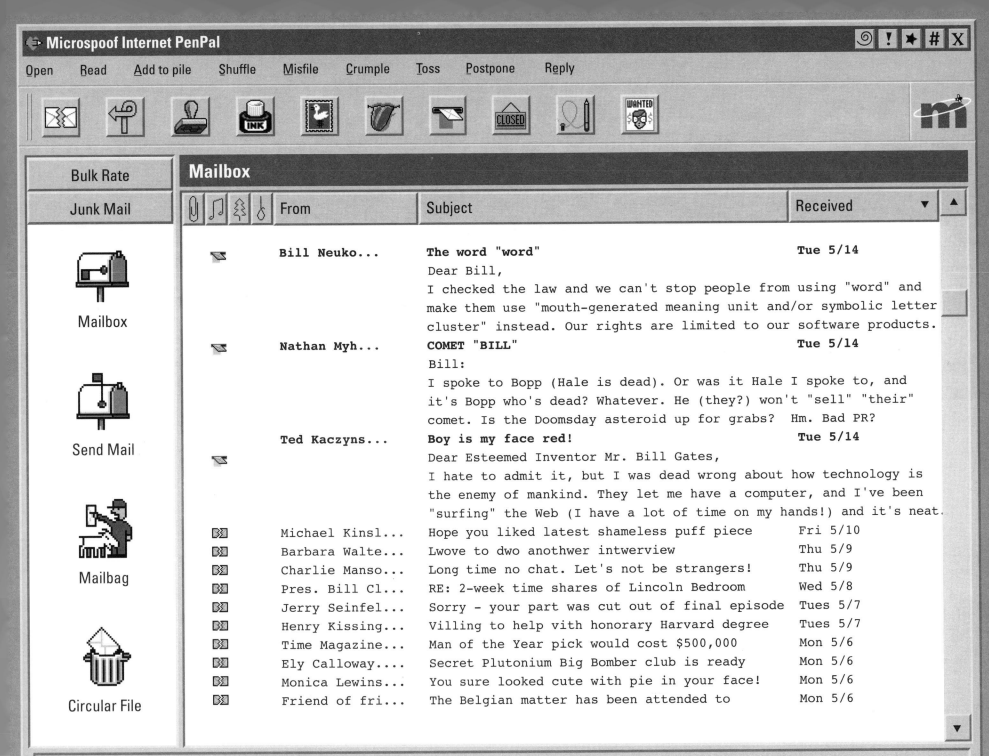

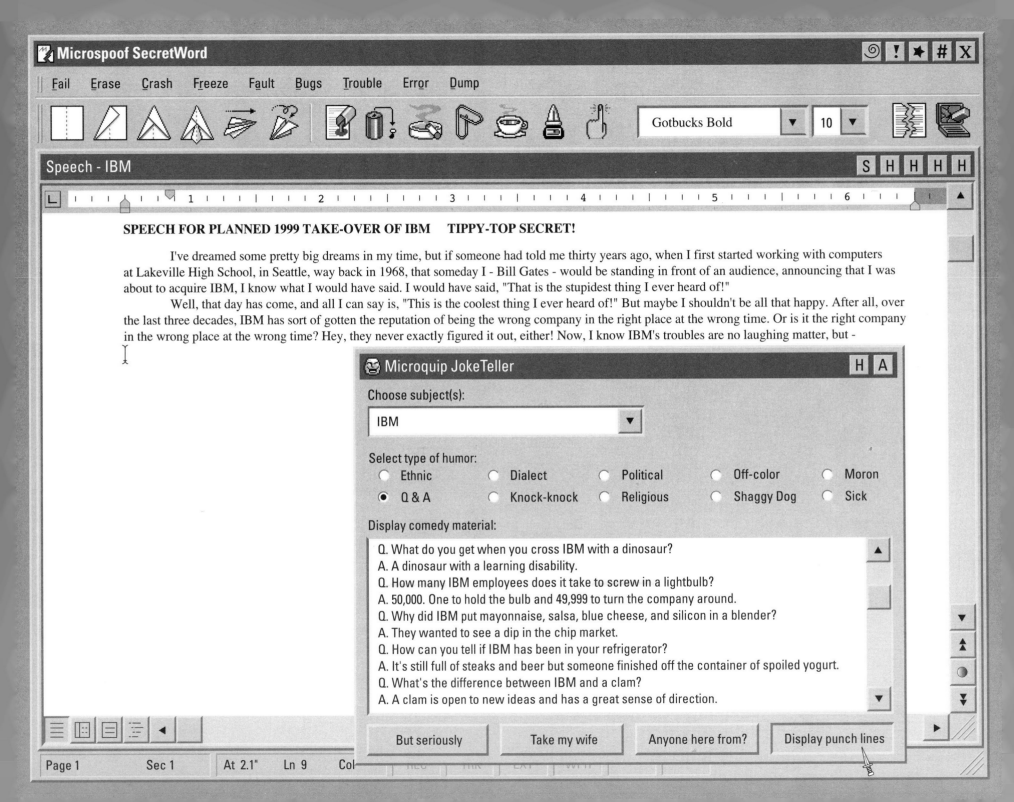

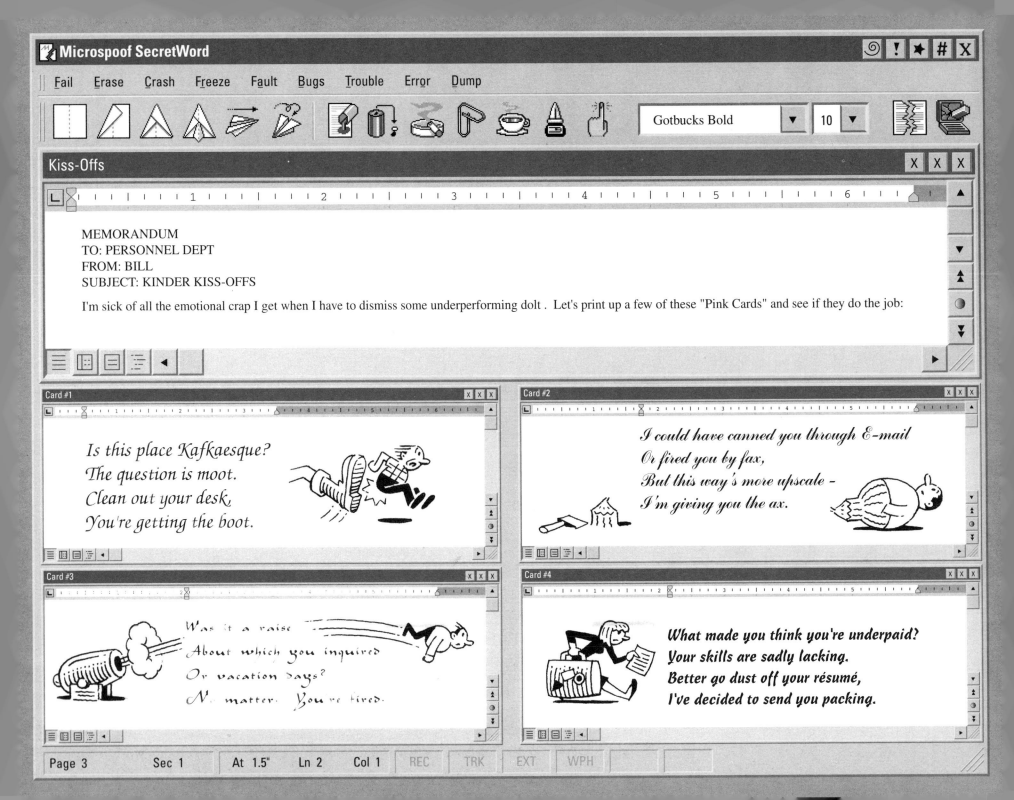

Microspoof SecretWord

Fail Erase Crash Freeze Fault Bugs Trouble Error Dump

Gotbucks Bold ▼ 10 ▼

Kiss-Offs

MEMORANDUM
TO: PERSONNEL DEPT
FROM: BILL
SUBJECT: KINDER KISS-OFFS

I'm sick of all the emotional crap I get when I have to dismiss some underperforming dolt . Let's print up a few of these "Pink Cards" and see if they do the job:

Card #1

Is this place Kafkaesque?
The question is moot.
Clean out your desk,
You're getting the boot.

Card #2

I could have canned you through E-mail
Or fired you by fax,
But this way's more upscale –
I'm giving you the ax.

Card #3

Was it a raise
About which you inquired
Or vacation days?
No matter. You're fired.

Card #4

What made you think you're underpaid?
Your skills are sadly lacking.
Better go dust off your résumé,
I've decided to send you packing.

Page 3   Sec 1   At 1.5"   Ln 2   Col 1   REC   TRK   EXT   WPH

Imprinted Advertising Specialties to Boost Sales or Build Morale

FAKE CRACKED MONITOR - Adheres to screen. Custom imprinted. Choose: Bullet holes or blunt object bash.

MILLIE, THE MILLENNIUM BUG - Cheer up employees' computers with this fuzzy, adorable reminder of the disaster to come.

DRINK CADDY - Handsome holder fits most cans, cups, bottles. Your ad copy, always logged on.

PRODUCTIVITY - ENHANCING CALENDAR - No Saturdays, Sundays or holidays. Each week has 9 days. Imprint right away - Sir!

JUMBO PEN - Mar-resistant finish. Fits in most cubicles.

OFFICE PET! - LOVABLE ANOLIS LIZARD - A living reminder of your generosity. Inflatable throat sac, fly-catching capability. **FREE IMPRINT ON QUANTITIES OVER 1000!**

KRASH KIT - Customers and employees will know you care! Contains 2 flares, distress sign, fire extinguisher and snack in a leather-tone bag.

MIRACLE MAGIC SPONGE - Grows 3000 times its size when wet. So does your goodwill message!

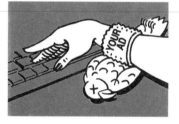

CTS PREVENTER - Lab tests proved that a pigeon is the ideal under-wrist orthotic. We found thousands of surplus birds, euthanized them and preserved them. Imprinted terry wrist strap included.

ORDER FORM

Yes, I want to build business and/or boost morale.

Item #	Quantity	Price

Shipping

Total

Imprint

Name

Address

E-mail

Credit Card #

Credit Card Type ▾

Gotbucks Bold   ▼   10   ▼

Confidential Memorandum

CONFIDENTIAL MEMORANDUM
TO: ALL
FROM: BILL

All too often we've spelled out our so-called "anticompetitive" strategies in internal documents that are then leaked or subpoenaed. From now on, use the following acronyms for these common business practices.

DATBOOB	Drive all the bastards out of business	PARPAYLAPOOD	Promote a rival product and you lose a place on our desktop
UTPUTCU	Undercut their prices until they cry Uncle!	PTOASTU	Pay them off and shut them up
CIBMILLWHIF	Clone it, but make it look like we had it first	HATTPAGATS	Hire all their top people and grab all their secrets
SICTMUTS	Slip in code that messes up their software	TTUFYWAPL	Tie them up for years with a phony lawsuit
AIRONEP	Announce imminent release of nonexistent product	BASSNOGAPOOMS	Bundle all software so no one gets a piece of our market share
BTOBTO	Beat them or buy them out	DADDAO	Dump all damaging documents at once
TACOS	Take, acquire, copy, or steal	LYSHO	Lie your silly head off
SASASAP	Smash all start-ups as soon as possible	SASASLOM	Suffer a sudden and severe loss of memory
MEDONDAA	Make exclusive deals or no deal at all	OGITWEP	Our goal is the whole enchilada, period
LAOSOYCHA	License all our software or you can't have any	WWIAAWWIN	We want it all, and we want it now

| | | | | | | | | | | | | | Gotbucks Bold ▼ | 10 ▼ | | |

Confidential Memorandum   e = m c²

L | | | | | 1 | | | | | | 2 | | | L | 3 | | | | | 4 | | | | | L5 | | | | | 6 | | |

CONFIDENTIAL MEMORANDUM

FROM: TECH SUPPORT

TO: BILL

SUBJECT: SECRET SHORTCUT KEYS

When our latest software is connected to the appropriate networks these functions can be triggered:

To Do This	Press This
Add a zero to your tax refund	Ctrl+Alt+Insert+Spacebar+F6
Remove a zero from your home's tax assessed value	Ctrl+Alt+Backspace+Home+Esc
Enhance past academic achievements	Ctrl+Backspace+A+Tab+Enter
Edit medical records	Alt+M+Spacebar+F4+Esc
Revise credit history	Shift+Esc+Delete+C+Spacebar
Invalidate a parking and/or speeding ticket	Alt+N+Shift+Tab+Insert
Remove points from your driver's license	Shift+Alt+End+F9+Enter
Expunge record of convictions	Ctrl+Shift+X+Spacebar+Delete
Pass an annual automobile inspection	Atl+Enter+A+Spacebar+Esc
Transpose digits in a taxpayer identification number	Alt+Shift+T+Insert+Enter
Delete your name from the jury duty list	Ctrl+Alt+Delete+Esc+F4
Qualify for an exemption from applicable sales taxes	Ctrl+Esc+Shift+Q+End
Waive annual registration fees	Alt+Shift+Delete+W+F6
Cancel a scheduled IRS audit	Ctrl+Alt+Shift+Esc+Delete+F9
Alter a meter reading	Alt+M+Spacebar+Shift+F2
Triple your frequent flier miles	Ctrl+Insert+F+Tab+F3
Change vote totals in a local election	Ctrl+Alt+Shift+Z+Home+F7
Execute a stock transaction at yesterday's price	Ctrl+Shift+D+J+Spacebar+F8
Insert loopholes in standard contracts	Ctrl+Insert+Shift+L+Enter
Modify specifications in a previous patent application	Alt+Shift+P+Insert+End
Obtain a CIA "Top Secret" security clearance	Ctrl+Alt+K+Shift+Esc
Get a reservation in a hot restaurant on short notice	Alt+Enter+Insert+R+Shift+F5
Book the first golf tee time at any course in the U.S.	Ctrl+T+Shift+Insert+Enter+G
Have yourself paged in every Planet Hollywood	Ctrl+Alt+Spacebar+H+Tab

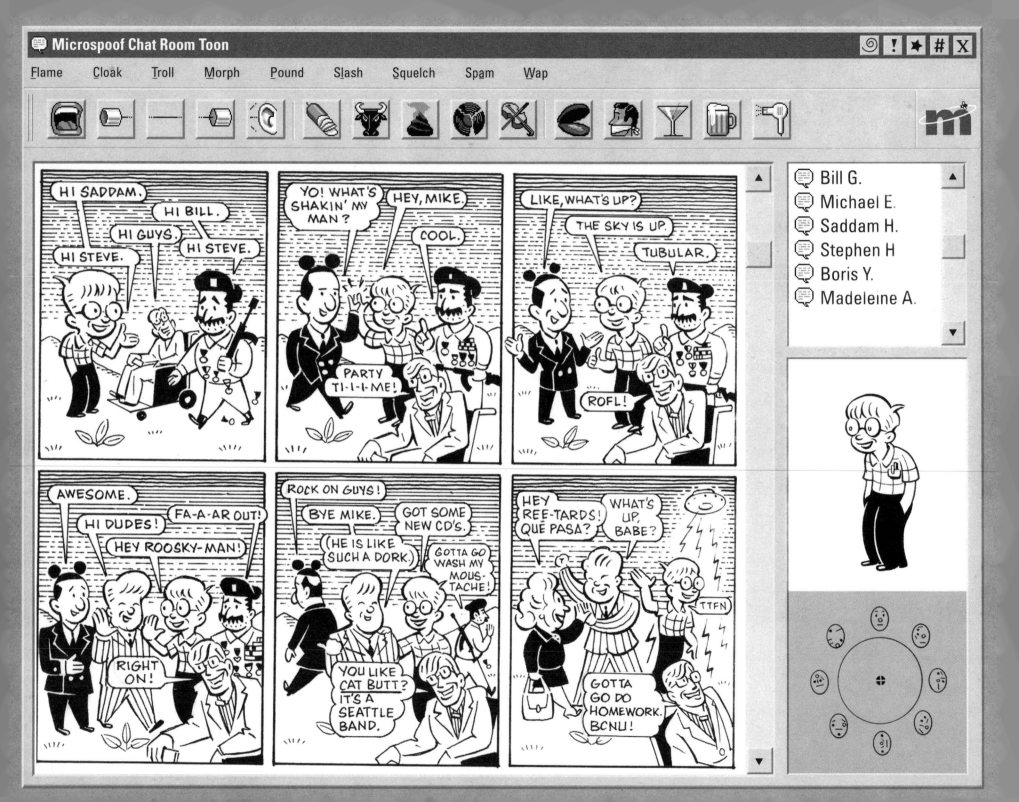

Fail   Erase   Crash   Freeze   Fault   Bugs   Trouble   Error   Dump

Gotbucks Bold ▼   10 ▼

Confidential Memorandum   D -

CONFIDENTIAL MEMORANDUM
TO: ALL PROGRAMMERS
FROM: BILL
SUBJECT: ERROR MESSAGES

Guys:
We've got to come up with tons of new on-screen error messages so users will blame themselves for foul-ups and glitches that were actually caused
by all the bugs in our latest software. Here are some possibilities, but we need a lot more:

Microspoof SecretWord ✓

System will not respond to your typed commands.
Your fingernails are too long.

Microspoof SecretWord ✓

Your document contained data too trivial
or frivolous to save in memory.
File has been deleted.

Microspoof SecretWord ✓

This file or folder is under a stack of other
files or folders and cannot be opened now.
Try again later.

Microspoof SecretWord ✓

The document you are seeking was used
to wipe up a data overflow on your hard
disk. It is no longer legible.

Microspoof SecretWord ✓

You have asked a silly question.
You are a dimwit.
No response will be provided.

Microspoof SecretWord ✓

The program is tired of making your stupid changes.
System is shutting down.

Microspoof SecretWord ✓

No such file was found in the folder.
Have you been drinking?

Microspoof SecretWord ✓

The filename you have chosen triggered
a bad memory. Select another name.

Microspoof SecretWord ✓

The file or folder you referred to is hidden somewhere
in your cache memory. You have 3 guesses.

Microspoof SecretWord ✓

This Help program is not designed for lazy or
incompetent users unable or unwilling to help
themselves. Get lost.

Microspoof SecretWord ✓

The command you entered is idiotic.
Program will not run if operated by a moron.

Microspoof SecretWord ✓

Your guesses were invalid.
File or folder has been deleted.
Better luck next time.

Microspoof SecretWord ✓

The system was not shut down properly last time.
Your punishment is a selective loss of data.

Microspoof SecretWord ✓

The file or folder you referred to cannot be found.
You must have left a window open and it fell out.

Microspoof SecretWord ✓

Overuse of filename extensions has caused a slipped
disk. The data responsible has been excised.

Page 1   Sec 1   At   Ln   Col   REC   TRK   EXT   WPH

Microspoof SecretWord - Artist rendering / Microspoof Home of Tomorrow

Fail   Erase   Crash   Freeze   Fault   Bugs   Trouble   Error   Dump

Gotbucks Bold   10

YOU EATING AGAIN, FATSO?

RAZZ!

12 point
10 point
8 point ab

① The brains of the operating system
② Voice synthesizing refrigerator
③ Face Maker 4.0
④ Burn Perfect 8.0
⑤ Drunkstation 5.0 Mixware
⑥ Prank 2000
⑦ Spreadsheet Pro
⑧ Workstation-on-a-Stick
⑨ Bath Planner '98

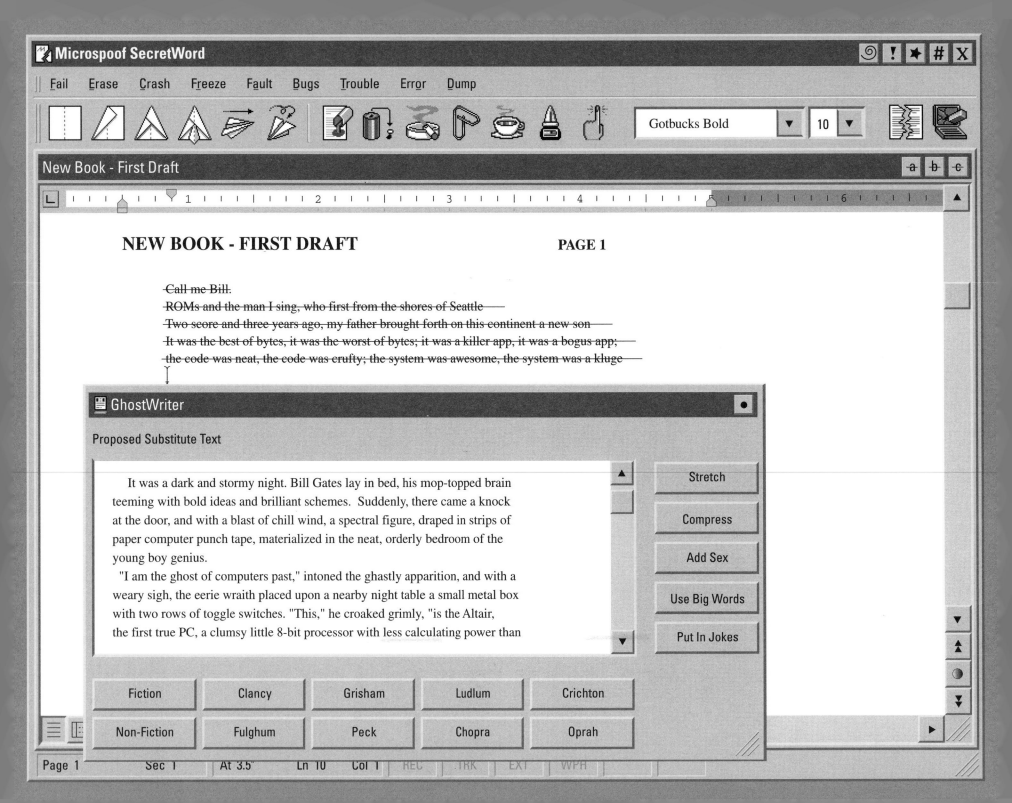

Gotbucks Bold   10

Ways to Discourage Stupid Calls to Microspoof Consumer Help Line

Ways to Discourage Stupid Calls to Microspoof Consumer Help Line

- Set up annoying multiple-option menu list. "If your description of the difficulty you have encountered contains more vowels than consonants, press 1"; "If your problem rhymes with 'air,' 'isk,' or 'ouse,' press 2"; "If the sum of the letters in your name is greater than 14, press 3"; etc.

- Buy rights to irritating background music when customers are on hold:
  - theme from "Poseidon Adventure"
  - Ravel's "Bolero"
  - "Itsy Bitsy Teenie Weenie Yellow Polkadot Bikini"
  - Joan Baez's version of "Michael, Row the Boat Ashore"
  - "Puff the Magic Dragon"
  - Philip Glass's "Einstein on the Beach" (all 6 hours)
  - Top hits of Soviet Army Chorus and Band

- Use 800 numbers no one can remember or everyone always remembers wrong or really would like to forget:

800 - GET-HILP	800 - ISH-KBOB	800 - BUG-GUTS
800 - COM-PEUT	800 - Z2B-4GOT	800 - EYE-STAB
800 - PRO-BLUM	800 - WET-SNOT	800 - ZIT-POPS

- Get a whole bunch of parrots and train them to squawk: "RELOAD WINDOWS AND TRY AGAIN" or "REBOOT, REBOOT"

- Contract with heavy-breathing sex-line service to handle jerks who insist on talking to a "human being" instead of a robot.

- Route calls through a pair of cheap discount-store toy walkie-talkies mounted on either end of a cage full of monkeys.

- Work with telephone co. to find way to give mild electric shock or earsplitting whine when caller asks stupid question.

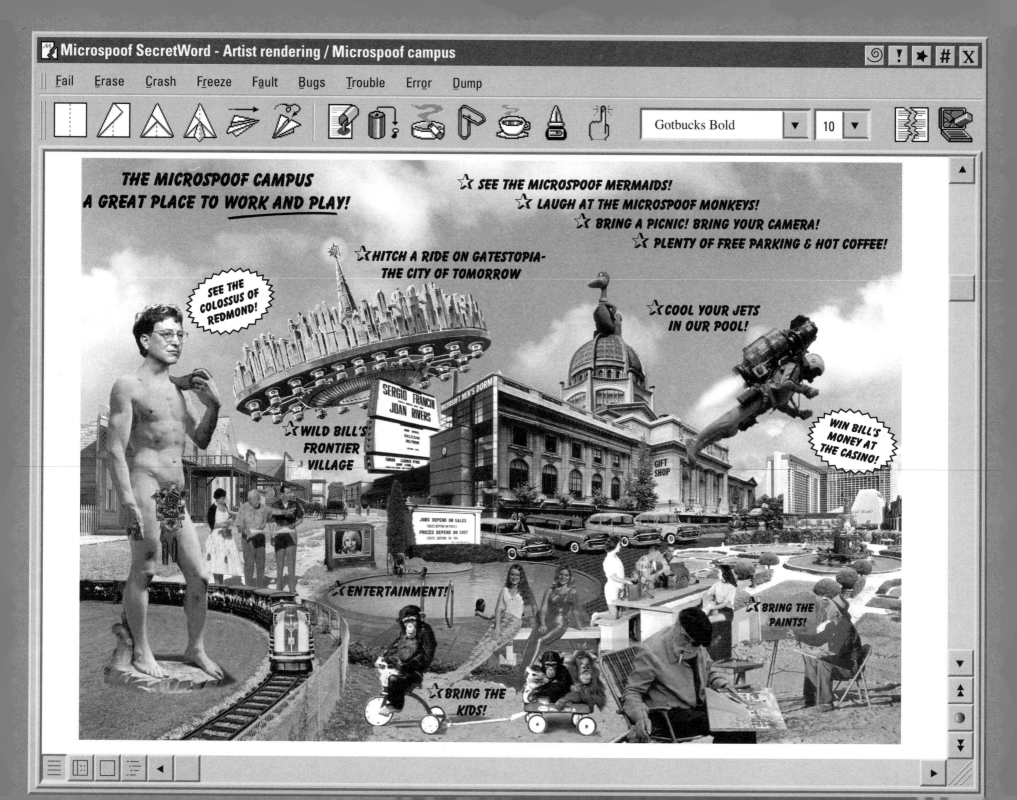

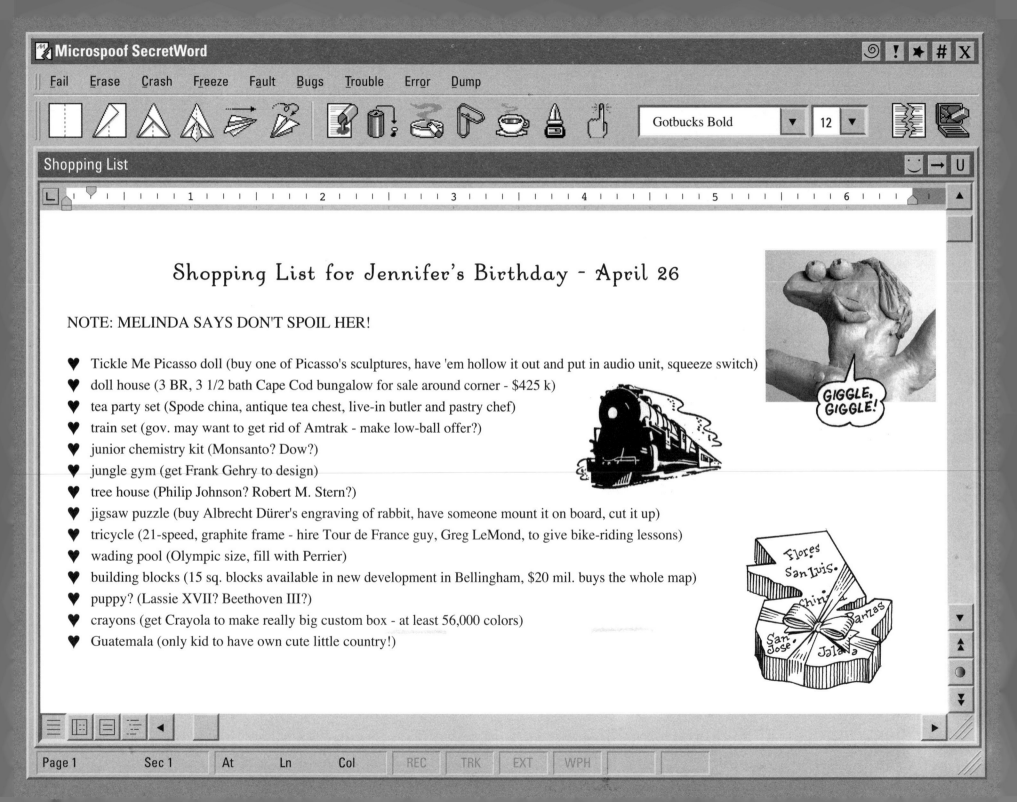

Microspoof SecretWord

Fail   Erase   Crash   Freeze   Fault   Bugs   Trouble   Error   Dump

Gotbucks Bold   12

Shopping List

Shopping List for Jennifer's Birthday - April 26

NOTE: MELINDA SAYS DON'T SPOIL HER!

- Tickle Me Picasso doll (buy one of Picasso's sculptures, have 'em hollow it out and put in audio unit, squeeze switch)
- doll house (3 BR, 3 1/2 bath Cape Cod bungalow for sale around corner - $425 k)
- tea party set (Spode china, antique tea chest, live-in butler and pastry chef)
- train set (gov. may want to get rid of Amtrak - make low-ball offer?)
- junior chemistry kit (Monsanto? Dow?)
- jungle gym (get Frank Gehry to design)
- tree house (Philip Johnson? Robert M. Stern?)
- jigsaw puzzle (buy Albrecht Dürer's engraving of rabbit, have someone mount it on board, cut it up)
- tricycle (21-speed, graphite frame - hire Tour de France guy, Greg LeMond, to give bike-riding lessons)
- wading pool (Olympic size, fill with Perrier)
- building blocks (15 sq. blocks available in new development in Bellingham, $20 mil. buys the whole map)
- puppy? (Lassie XVII? Beethoven III?)
- crayons (get Crayola to make really big custom box - at least 56,000 colors)
- Guatemala (only kid to have own cute little country!)

GIGGLE, GIGGLE!

Page 1   Sec 1   At   Ln   Col   REC   TRK   EXT   WPH

Address: http://www.sore_loser.com

SCORE 001   CARDS LEFT 5794387

NINJA BUSINESS CARDS

WALNUT CREMES: 3

CARAMEL QUEST

POODLES: 8   YORKIES: 6

VOLLEY DOG

SKILL LEVEL: BAREFOOT

STREET WALKIN' MAN

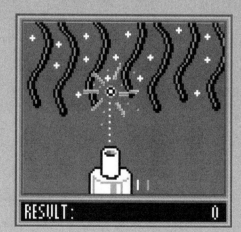

RESULT: 0

DANDERGEDDON

TURBULENCE: 8.1

PEOPLE, KNOCKING ON DOOR: 25

JET LAV

Microscam Excess

Fudge   Juggle   Kite   Doctor   Fake   Concoct   Backdate   Cook   Diddle/fiddle

FORMULA: Value of my time computed on basis of annual income = $43.78 per second

	A	B	C	D	E	F	G
1	Hidden Cost of My Nonproductive Activities During Work Week						
2	Activity	Duration	Cost per act	Daily frequency	Annual cost		
3	Rocking back & forth (per rock)	2.1 secs	$ 91.94	8,000	$ 73,550.40		
4	Checking stock market price	3.3 secs	144.47	2,000	28,894.80		
5	Pushing glasses up nose	1.3 secs	56.91	200	11,382.80		
6	Retying shoelaces (per shoe)	4.2 secs	183.88	15	2,758.14		
7	Removing spot from shirt	1 min 31 secs	3983.98	4	15,935.92		
8	Cleaning nails with paperclip	8.5 secs	372.13	6	2,232.75		
9	Picking nose (per nostril)	6.3 secs	275.81	10	27,581.14		
10	Brushing off dandruff	11.4 secs	499.09	500	24,954.60		
11	Sneezing	2.0 secs	96.32	15	1,444.74		
12	Farting (SBD)	3.2 secs	153.23	40	6,129.20		
13	Farting (Fudgie)	5.6 secs	245.17	2	490.33		
14	Zit patrol (per squeeze)	1 min 11 secs	3108.38	12	37,300.56		
15	Pocket pool	3 mins 41 secs	9675.38	5	48,376.90		
16							
17			Total annual cost = $65,897,088.00				
18							
19							
20							
21							

Sheet 1

Observe   Intrude   Penetrate   Probe   Survey   Eavesdrop   Monitor   Ogle

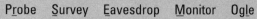

| Bug | Copy | Snapshot | Trapdoor | Wide Angle | Scramble | Cut Power | Exit |

Gain Access to: `All White House Computers`

Enter MicroSpy Code: `deep thought`

Unit	Location	User Name	Status
IBM300PL/233MHz/32mb/4.2gb	Oval Office	Bill Clinton	On line
Compaq6000/300MHz/32mb/4.3gb	East Wing	Al Gore	On line
IBM770/233MHz/32mb/4gb	West Wing	Michael McCurry	Off line
DellXPSD300/300MHz/128mb/9gb	Family Quarters	Hillary Clinton	Off line
HP-VL5/233MHz/32mb/4gb	East Wing	John Podesta	On line
Gateway8002/233MHz/64mb/4gb	East Wing	Sidney Blumenthal	On line
AST-MST/300MHz/32mb/4gb	Basement	James Carville	On line
IBM300GL/233MHz/32mb/2.5gb	Basement	Robert Bennett	On line
HP-E40/266MHz/32mb/4.2gb	West Wing	David Kendall	On line
Compaq4000/266MHz/32mb/3.2gb	West Wing	Bruce Lindsey	Off line
MicronXKU/300MHz/64mb/4gb	Basement	Paul Begala	On line
Acer200MHz/32mb/2.1gb	Cabinet Room		On line
IBM300PL200MHz/32mb/2.5gb	Press Room		Off line
CTX760MT166MHz/16mb/2gb	Basement		Off line
HP-Brio8172/166MHz/16mb/2.1gb	Basement		

Peeping Tom wants to know what you'd like to do?

● Activate hidden screen camera

○ Activate hidden microphone

○ Activate speakers

● Read lips

○ Just visiting

| Gotcha! | Run | Hide |

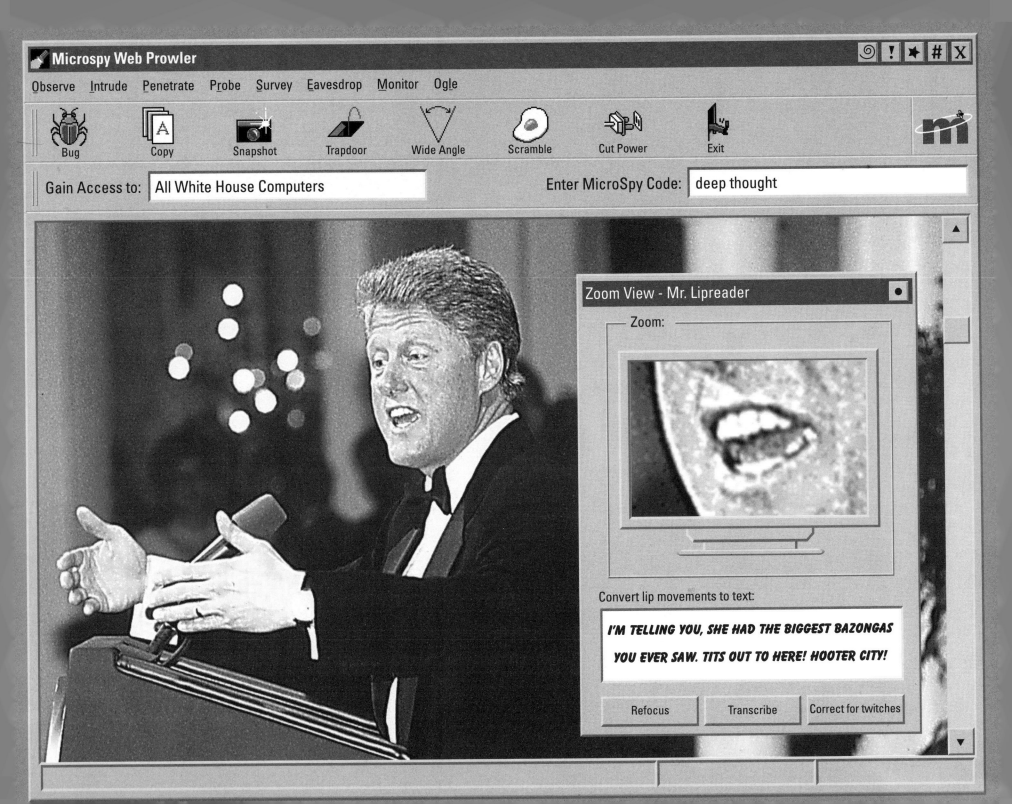

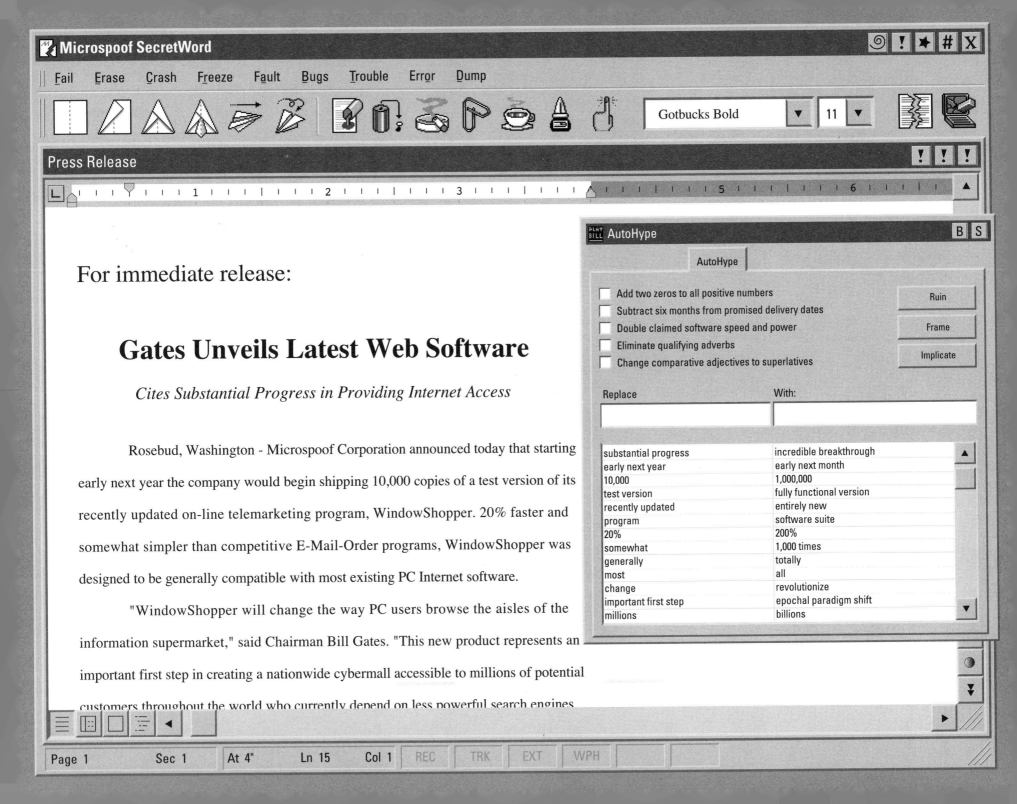

page 5

CAPT. JANEWAY
Wait, there is one thing we could do. We could use the Temporal Wave Tachyon Flux to energize the wormhole and beam Bill Gates aboard the Enterprise from earth in the 21st century. He's the only man brilliant enough to get us out of this Temporal Restraining Field.

CHAKOTAY
You're right, Captain. With his towering intellect, he might just be able to come up with some incredibly ingenious method of countering the brain-smothering effects of the Innovation Damping Warp Vortex the Renojanets have constructed in hyperspace.

HOLODOC
Bill Gates - wasn't he considered the Leonardo da Vinci of his age?

TUVOK
That is not a valid parallel. Compared to Gates, da Vinci was nothing more than a small-time tinkerer.

HOLODOC
It could be risky - if the Superluminal Synchronic Transfer encounters any local Zeta-Phase Paradoxes, Gates could end up as just so much static in the quantum matrix.

CAPT. JANEWAY
Gates was known for his enormous personal courage. I'm sure he'd want us to try. Bridge to Transporter Room.
Prepare to engage!

Microspiff VirtualValet

PLAY BILL

⟳ ! ★ # X

Fold   Press   Polish   Buff   Hover   Bow   Scrape   Pander   Truckle

StyleSetter Fashion Statement ●

| Ties | Shirts | Pants | Jackets | Glasses | Socks | Shoes | Underwear | Other |

Select Neckwear Pattern:

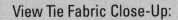

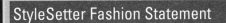

View Tie Fabric Close-Up:

Apply Food Stain

Add Nasal Debris

Wrinkle

Unravel Threads

Use to Wipe Glasses

Make Thin End Longer   Tuck Fat End in Belt   Display Clip-on Version   Bolo Options

Fail   Erase   Crash   Freeze   Fault   Bugs   Trouble   Error   Dump

Gotbucks Bold   12

The Republic of Bill

The Republic of Bill

HEAD OF STATE: Der Billmeister, El Microsupremo, The Gator!
CAPITAL: Plenty!
GOVERNMENT: Keep out!
LANGUAGES: English, Basic
MOTTO: MIHI MIHI OMNES SUNT - "It's mine - all mine"
ANTHEM:
My country 'tis of me,
Neat land of yours truly,
Of me I sing.
Land where I'm number one,
And work is so much fun,
Let's hear it everyone,
Bill is the king!
FLAG: Stars 'n' Bars
CURRENCY: The dollar "Bill" !

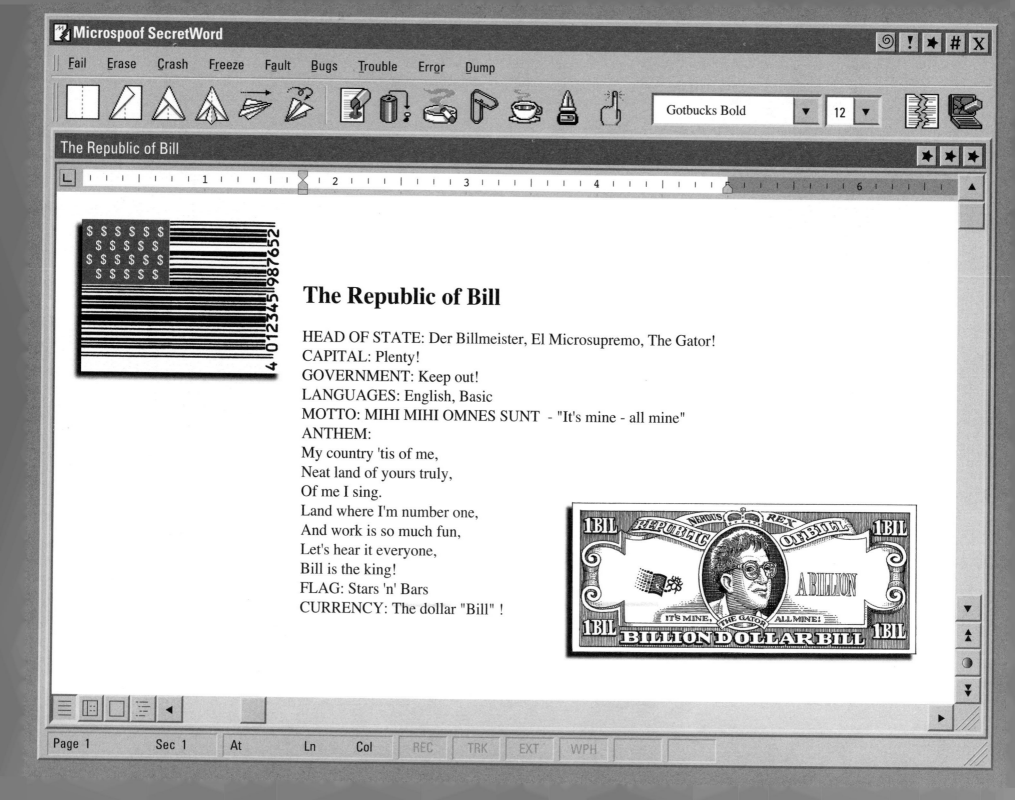

Page 1   Sec 1   At   Ln   Col   REC   TRK   EXT   WPH

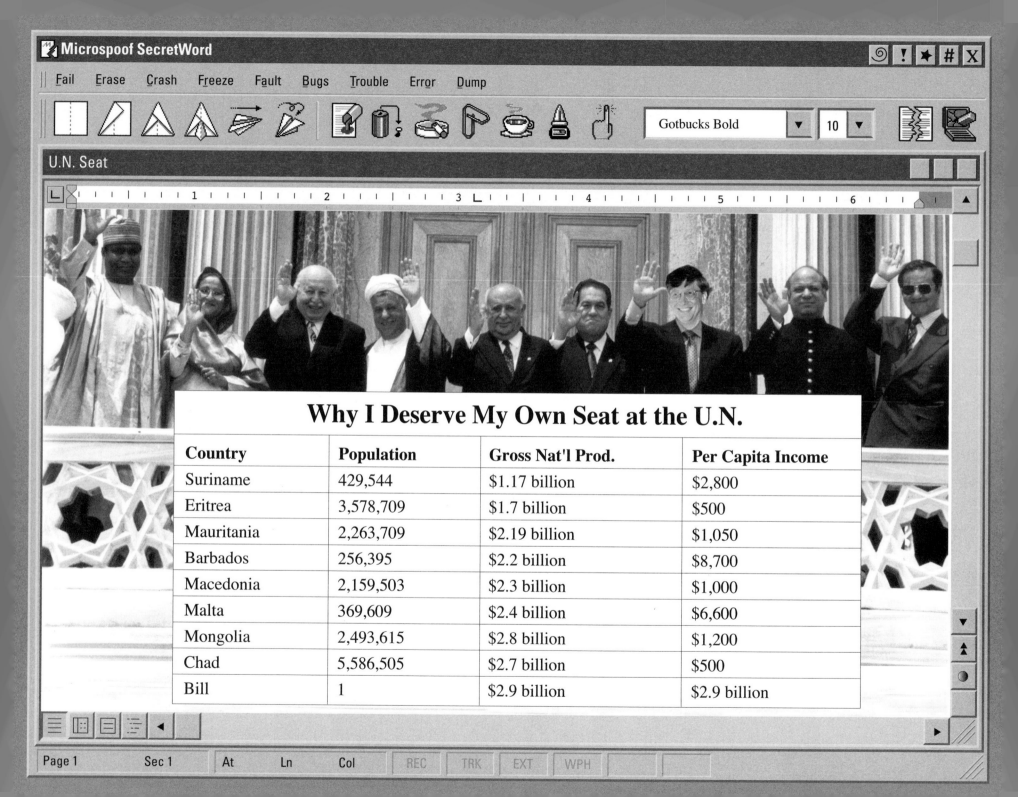

Microspoof SecretWord

Fail   Erase   Crash   Freeze   Fault   Bugs   Trouble   Error   Dump

Gotbucks Bold   10

U.N. Seat

Why I Deserve My Own Seat at the U.N.

Country	Population	Gross Nat'l Prod.	Per Capita Income
Suriname	429,544	$1.17 billion	$2,800
Eritrea	3,578,709	$1.7 billion	$500
Mauritania	2,263,709	$2.19 billion	$1,050
Barbados	256,395	$2.2 billion	$8,700
Macedonia	2,159,503	$2.3 billion	$1,000
Malta	369,609	$2.4 billion	$6,600
Mongolia	2,493,615	$2.8 billion	$1,200
Chad	5,586,505	$2.7 billion	$500
Bill	1	$2.9 billion	$2.9 billion

Page 1   Sec 1   At   Ln   Col   REC   TRK   EXT   WPH